A Sense of Science
Exploring Electricity

Claire Llewellyn

W
FRANKLIN WATTS
LONDON · SYDNEY

This edition 2012
First published by
Franklin Watts
338 Euston Road
London NW1 3BH

Franklin Watts Australia
Hachette Children's Books
Level 17/207 Kent Street
Sydney NSW 2000

Editor: Jeremy Smith
Art Director: Jonathan Hair
Design: Matthew Lilly
Cover and design concept:
Jonathan Hair
Photography: Ray Moller except:
Alamy: 10b, 25t,
Corbis: 6, 11t, 13b, 17b.

We would like to thank Scallywags for
their help with the models in this book.

A CIP catalogue record
for this book is available
from the British Library.

Dewey classification: 537

ISBN: 978 1 4451 0635 9

Printed in China

Franklin Watts is a division of
Hachette Children's Books,
an Hachette UK company.
www.hachette.co.uk

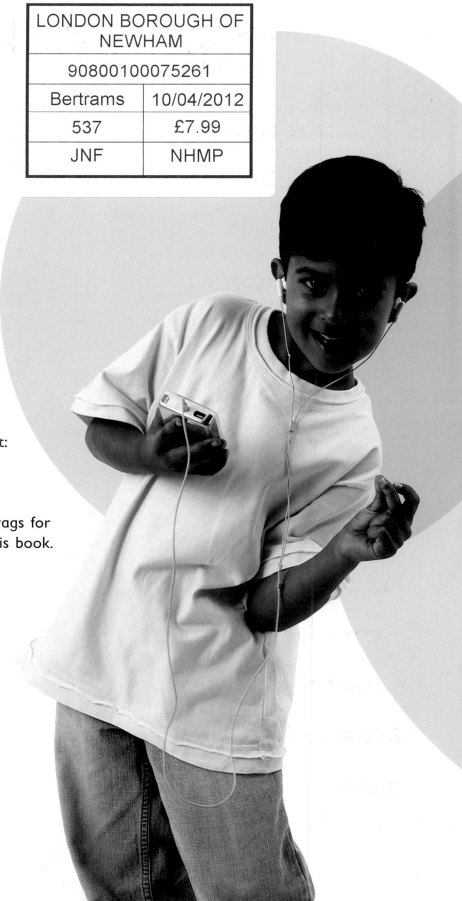

Contents

We use electricity   6

Electric light   8

Electric heat   10

Electric machines   12

Making sound   14

In the mains   16

Looking at batteries   18

Making a circuit   20

On and off   22

Electrical parts   24

Electricity is dangerous   26

Glossary   28

Activity: Make a circuit   29

Index   30

We use electricity

We use electricity every day.

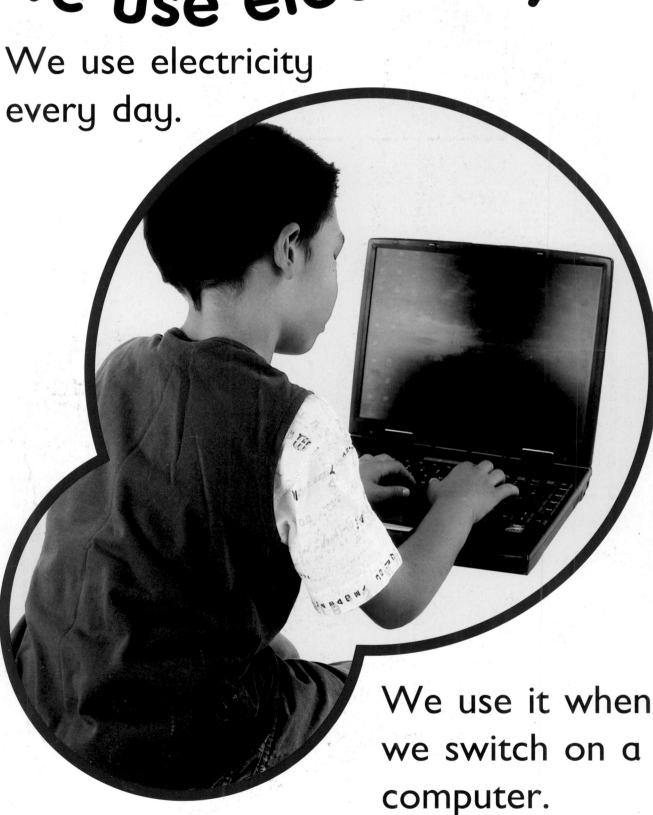

We use it when we switch on a computer.

We use electricity to turn a stereo on.

All electric

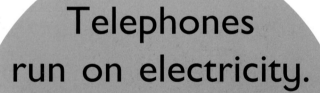

Look around you. Can you see something that runs on electricity?

Telephones run on electricity.

Electric light

Electricity
gives us light.

We switch
on lights when
it gets dark
so that we
can see.

Street lights come on at night.

See the light
With a grown-up, light a candle in the dark. Then switch on an electric light. How are the two lights different?

A car's headlights use electricity.

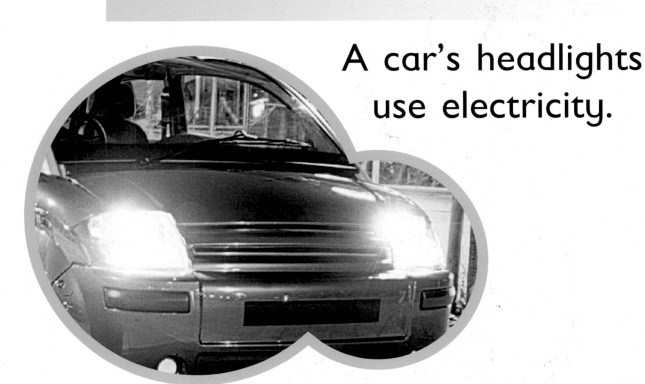

Electric heat

Electricity gives us heat.

Hot stuff

With an adult, switch on a machine that gives out heat. What changes do you notice? What happens when you switch it off?

A microwave heats up food.

Electricity makes an iron hot.

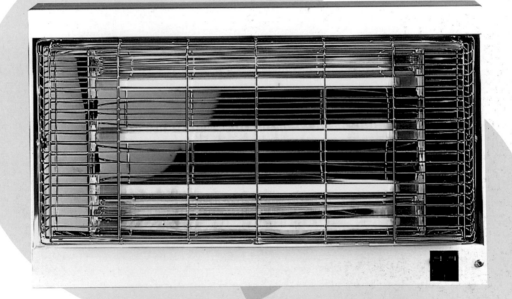

An electric fire heats a room.

Electric machines

Many machines
run on electricity.

A fan
spins
round and
keeps us cool.

On the move

What happens when you switch on a hairdryer?
What happens when you switch it off?

A washing machine washes our dirty clothes.

Some people brush their teeth with an electric toothbrush.

Making sound

Some electric machines can make sounds.

We can play music on an MP3 player.

Loud or soft?

Switch on a radio. What happens?
What can you do to make the sound louder?
How can you make it softer?

We can hear our friend's voice on the telephone.

This keyboard works on electricity.

In the mains

Many electric machines have a plug that fits in a socket in the wall.

Mains electricity is dangerous. Never touch sockets in the wall.

This vacuum cleaner uses mains electricity.

Mains electricity is made in power stations.

It flows along wires and into our homes.

In the wire

With an adult, look at a piece of electric flex. What can you see inside?

Looking at batteries

Some electric machines run on batteries.

Battery play

Switch a torch on and off. Now find the batteries and take them out. What happens when you switch the torch on now?

Batteries are little stores of electricity.

When the batteries run out, we put new ones in or recharge the old ones.

Machines with batteries have no flex and are easy to move around.

Making a circuit

Electricity flows along a pathway called a circuit.

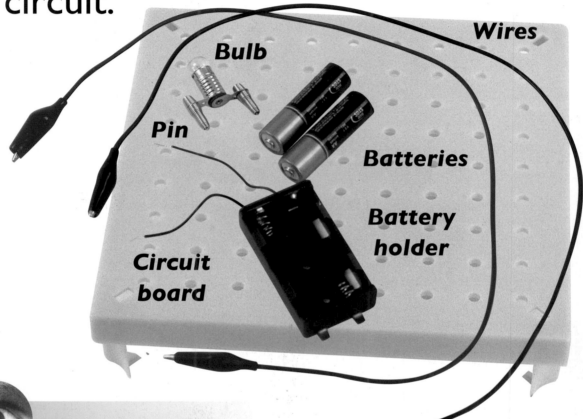

Wires

Bulb

Pin

Batteries

Battery holder

Circuit board

See the light

Look carefully at the light bulb. Can you see anything inside it?

We can make a circuit with a battery, two wires and a bulb.

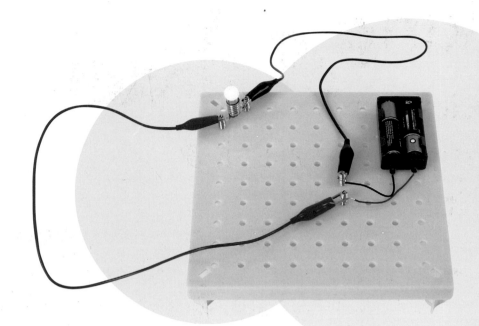

When we join all the bits in the circuit, the bulb lights up.

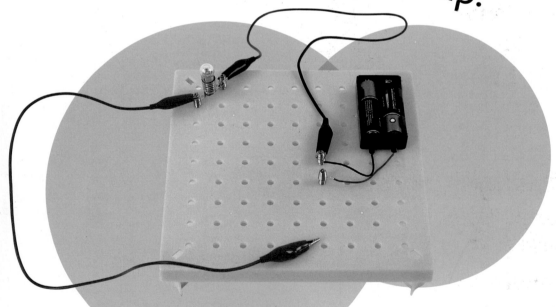

If there is a gap in the circuit, the bulb goes out.

On and off

Electricity flows into a machine when we switch it on.

If we push the button, the television switches on.

We press the switch to turn the toy on.

The electricity stops when we switch it off.

Where's the switch?

Have a look in your bathroom.
How do you turn the bathroom light on?
How do you turn it off?

Electrical parts

Electric machines have lots of different parts.

Around the house

Which room in your home has the most electric machines?

Bulb

Flex

These are the electric parts of a lamp.

These are the electric parts of a torch.

Bulb

Battery

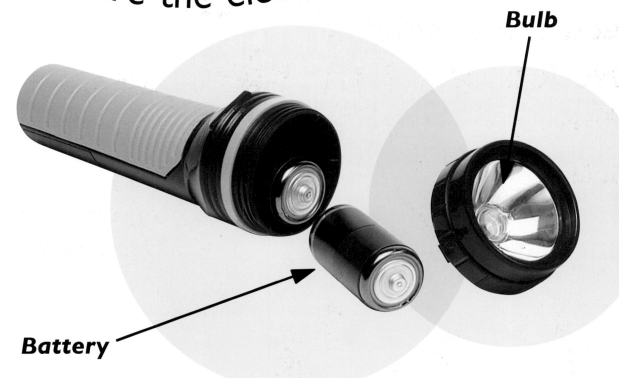

On/Off switch

These are the electric parts of a CD-player.

Speaker

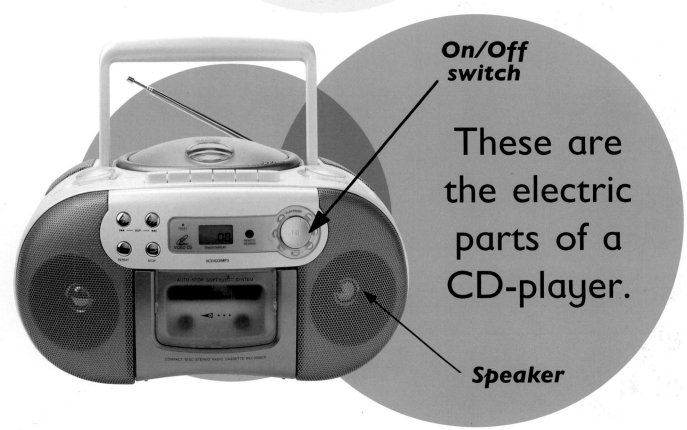

Electricity is dangerous

Electricity helps us in many ways but it can be very dangerous.

We must never play with plugs, sockets or wires.

Never play
near electricity
outside.

Batteries are
the safest way
to learn about
electricity.

Stay safe
Draw a sketch of your kitchen. Mark
the areas where you need to be careful
because of electricity.

Glossary

Battery

Store of electricity that can be used inside electric machines.

Bulb

The glass part of an electric lamp that gives out light.

Circuit

A loop that electricity can flow along.

Flex

The bendy wire found on machines that run on mains electricity.

Mains

Electricity that comes into our homes from power stations.

Power station

The place where electricity is made.

Plug

The part of an electrical machine that is put into a socket to get electricity from the mains.

Socket

A place in a wall designed for a plug to be inserted to receive mains electricity.

Switch

Something that starts or stops electricity flowing.

Make your own circuit

You will need a bulb, circuit board, wires, metal pins, batteries and a battery holder.

bulb

pin

battery

circuit board

wires

Set up your circuit to match the one on the left. Attach each wire to the bulb and the battery holder.

What happens if you unclip a wire and break the circuit?

Index

batteries 18, 19,
    20, 27, 29
bulb 20, 21, 24,
    25, 29

circuit 20, 21, 29

flex 17, 19, 24, 25

heat 10, 11

light 8, 9, 20, 21,
    23

machines 10, 11,
    12, 13, 14 , 16,
    18, 19, 22, 24
mains electricity 16,
    17

plug 16, 26
power station 17

socket 16, 26
sound 14, 15

wires 17, 20, 26, 29